Whispers Of Fortitude

Mastering The Battle Against Depression.

Arla P. Hopefield

TABLE OF CONTENT

INTRODUCTION

You think depression starts in a day? Hell no! Is something that builds up in a person gradually even without you knowing it. Come to think of it, have it ever cross your mind that most depression start from a particular attribute or character you refused to let go even when you know is not working? For instance, choosing the wrong opinion or the wrong sides of things continuously – maybe you get into an argument with a friend or family and each time this happens, you are always found in that loosing space while they win.

Look into this closely, can you now see the high chance of depression in this? Yes the chances are high because when you look around you, you see clearly the problems yet you choose to remain stubborn maintaining this perspective, you get depressed because your environment wont succumb neither you of which you happens to be the one at the loosing ends in every of this chase.

In other case maybe you give up easily even when you are doing the right thing. For instance, you are introduced to a kind of business to make money, along the line you feel things aren't going your way then you quit yet when you look around you, others involved are doing very well. This can result to a temporal sadness. As time goes, you try something different with great hopes and enthusiasm still you quit again, again and again. At this point you tend to start asking yourself questions like why me, what is wrong am I cursed? e.t.c. Without knowing that this could be as a result of the lack of patients. When at this level you can't find answers to this questions, that initial temporal sadness grows to become depression.

Even though there are other factors that can lead to depression, its best to know that which start with our personality. There are depressions caused by maltreatment at workplace by employer, marriage by husband or wife and many more, but remember they don't start in a day.it is something that cumulates until it gets to its peak you shouldn't let it get to that point.

CHAPTER 1: THAT DEPRESSED STATE

If there is anything you would want to know about depression is that it does not only controls the minds but fight to be in charge of your whole body from your head to your feet. You feel it like it's so close to you never leaving your side. You get to feel it moving inside you therefore causing you that unexplainable discomfort.

It can be controlling and demanding and the crazy thing is once this happens, you are left with no other choice but succumb to its desires. The annoying thing is that you sock your pillow with tears still no solution to move out of it. It gives you more reasons to cry and not a single way out. It leaves your mind in the most confusing state ever.

One moment you think you can explain how you feel the other moment you are back to square one.

For instance, you want to be with friends yet again they become your problem and you want to be left alone. Depression makes you want to do the most unthinkable thing you never imagined especially when it's entangled with loneliness.

A lot of people believe that loneliness is the main cause of these depression forgetting that it's at this lonely parts that all those features played in. The past only use loneliness as a stepping stone. Although depression manifests differently on different people, it doesn't change the fact that the feelings are discomforting.

Now get the point correctly not all lonely people are depressed you doubt? What about the introvert? Do you address them as depressed people? No of course you can be a kind of person that naturally prefer staying alone. This doesn't mean you are depressed it becomes depression the moment the mind has been messed up emotionally, mentally, psychologically and more , then loneliness comes in. You find yourself wanting to be alone just to cry with no solution.

It becomes dangerous when people around thinks you are perfectly fine. It is at this point in more severe cases, the suicidal thought plays in. You fake this smile when you are around others everything seems ok for the moment but deep down you are thinking of what happens next once you are alone again.

One thing to basically understand is that loneliness and depression are distinct concepts. Yes it is true that loneliness causes sadness also, at that moment you feel like being with someone most especially with the opposite sex maybe to love and to be loved but when you talk of depression, it feels like this heaviness suffocating you beneath the dark cloud you don't know where to start from.

It comes with persistence feelings of sadness, hopelessness and lack of interest in almost everything that comes your way. While loneliness can contribute to feelings of sadness, its temporal and not all lonely people are clinically depressed but just as stated earlier, depression is something that grows with time it is possible that loneliness can gradually become depression when it becomes a frequent occurrence.

You can describe depression as a moment of fear, fear of the unknown, what does the future holds, the fear of trying to balance struggle with questions like what if it still goes wrong? Fear that you might never be able to achieve a certain goal, fear that your time is gradually wailing out without anything tangible. Fear of existence, depression triggers existential concerns. You feel living is meaningless those beautiful things of the world becomes irrelevant in fact, problems to the mind. Absolutely nothing matters anymore. You even try to create a small world around this depressive circle, making a part of your pains becomes your peace. This is where this loneliness we talked about also comes to play here. You are seen always in isolation, because at that depressing state, that has become your peace of mind which is a problem.

Depression clouds the mind of different people in different ways. To some, fear is accompanied with social anxiety were you fear judgment, rejection or negative evaluation from others. Getting involve with people becomes very difficult. At a point, something that can be addressed as fear of self comes in. thoughts which may include self-critical and negative beliefs, leading to a fear of one's own thoughts and emotions. Different scary thoughts plays in your mind making you feel, that could be a way out of the depressed state. This fear has become one tool depression holds against its victims it messes with the mental health.

Sometimes, you see yourself trying to break free from depression in different ways like writing down those things you feel leads to that depressed state in the first place, burning it, trying to communicate with loved once, etc By so doing, you seem to get a bit of relieve or even feel better. Sometimes, you feel like you are better off in isolation.

These are all state of depressions at different level. Yes at every point in time, one gets that feelings of depression. Now, the big question is was there a room for it? Did you give space for this wondering disaster to dwell in you? One thing is sure, feelings sometimes, looks like they can't be defined especially in a very critical time involving the mind but this is where it all begins in the mind, that moment you can get hold of that feelings and thought blowing gentle whispers for you to understand before that depression sets into your mind controlling you. Let's look at chapter two were you probably understand the point to the term "Don't get depressed".

CHAPTER 2: DON'T GET DEPRESSED LISTEN!

Have you ever noticed this deep inner mind that communicate with you? No am not talking of some loud thoughts that randomly crosses the mind on different occasion. This one is different. It is recognized by few as the gentlest whisper any human can get from their heads. It speaks with you, tells you things, convince and many more. It works with your experiences in life to communicate with you.

A lot of people might feel they haven't ever come across such before while others knows of its existence – I mean they are sensitive enough to know of this communicative spirit but ignorantly pay less or zero attention to it. It usually don't persist but once listened to, you might feel rebuked.

It is always so calm. It tells you the right thing to do at all times it never fails you just need to listen.

Before you get into that depressing state, you were warned by this positive mind. It knows when things are going to affect you, it is always connected with your spirit and the physical wellbeing. Once this mind speaks and you listen, you don't fail. Therefore there is no room for depression. Depression works with failure. The moment you fail it start building in you. This mind though very tricky, protects you from that, only if you listen deeply. Let's use this illustration. It is of no doubt that most successful men listen more. Now pay attention, do you take note of the successful I used? It is the same thing when you listen closely to that positive mind. It knows when your next action will lead you to depression and warns you firmly on it.

In a situation where you are about to get something you have always wanted which you are willing to do anything for, it knows if that will later lead to depression it knows everything and its tells you ahead of time did you listen?. Even before you get too familiar with a particular personality, remember the positive mind works with experience. It studies you to know the personality around then it evaluate this with previous experience letting you see facts which you can only understands when you listen carefully.

It might shock you to know that in as much as depression attacks at any slight opportunity given, there are still a lot of people that has never been a victim to it. The easiest way to overcome depression is your ability to listen to your inner mind as mindful as possible. Let me make you understand better how this mind works. Because this mind is very positive at all times, it always tries to pass right information for your wellbeing.

Have you ever notice a circumstance whereby you have to deal with certain issues along the line you feel your conscience is pushing you to a particular step to follow but you ignored and follow another step. In some cases this mind might become push a little, you feel the heaviness and then you know this was the wrong step to go. Immediately you correct that step you feel peace in your mind. Yes this might have occurred several times.

Listening is the key to fight depression at all times. Before you get to that level of depression, the positive mind has informed you. When you hear it tell you things, you know it is the one speaking to you because it works with your experiences. It is that same mind that gives you deep inspirations, guides and teaches. This positive mind those not let you control it like you do with other parts of your body. Sometimes you are aware of this mind but you want it to work your own way. At that points it shifts. It can't be controlled.

A lot of people prefer to follow emotions than facing reality. It is important to strike a balance between acknowledging and understanding ones emotions and realizing the objective reality of a situation. Over reliance on distorted or negative emotions without a realistic assessment of the situation can contribute to feelings of hopelessness or helplessness, which are of course associated with depression.

Healthy emotional regulation involves acknowledging emotions while also critically evaluating and responding to the actual circumstances. The safest way to critically evaluate and respond to circumstances is by listening to the positive mind in you. Don't say you don't have it, you just haven't given yourself the time to listen to it.

Once you start paying quality attention, it becomes like someone is physically talking to you because it becomes a frequent occurrence you always listen to. If a situation comes up, the positive mind leads you to do the right thing.

Depression doesn't go with doing the right thing. Many people fall victims because thy deviate to things they feel or create to be right for them unfortunately, this positive mind don't work this way. It doesn't controls yet won't let you control it. More reason why is unique and can be able to detect troubles that can lead to depression.

It can be a bit challenging to get in touch strongly with this positive mind if you are easily distracted by emotions. The problem is that people tends to only recognize this voice when they are left with no other option or person to turn to or cry to. Forgetting that this positive mind is both there when you have people around and when you don't, it evaluate and doesn't ignore. It is easier to be calm when you are sad than when you aren't sad.

Unfortunately even while sad, the probability to listen to the positive mind is slim. Why because you get carried away with other things that could cause you depression like revenge, pity, stubbornness and many more therefore preventing this positive mind from communicating to you. It can't work with these distractions in your mind.

If you want to fight depression, the first thing to do is to be calm, even when angry, sad etc then you listen, listen deep and carefully, don't work with emotions because emotions might give you ideas that will later lead to a depressing state so just listen!

CHAPTER 3 LET LOOSE WHILE JOY CONTROLS

We all have that potential to choose were we drive genuine joy or choose things that seems to bring joy while in the real sense, they don't. It is difficult for depression to temper with a genuine happy mind. In as much that many circumstances can lead to depression, joy isn't part. First let's define joy and understand what it means. Joy is a profound and positive emotion characterized by a deep sense of happiness, contentment and delight.

It often arises from experiences that brings a sense of fulfillment, satisfaction and connection. Joy is more enduring than fleeting happiness and can be found in meaningful relationships, personal accomplishment, or moments of gratitude. It contributes to an overall sense of wellbeing and can positively impact both mental and physical health.

In chapter two, we addressed the positive mind in connection to depression and how to listen to this mind in order not to even have any stages of depression. And as stated that depression can't penetrate if joys occupies. Now this positive mind that we are all privilege to have, tries to make sure our inner joy is preserved at all times when we listen. On a real practical sense. You must have come across certain times when you listen, that you have joy inside you or your existing joy remains.

As in the definition of joy, it is a profound and positive emotion characterized by a deep sense of happiness, contentment and delight.

Like the positive mind, joy is a positive emotion that takes over you when something is apparently going right or as planned. Now, that thing that went right was probably fueled by the positive mind therefore the space which would have been occupied by depression, become replaced with your inner joy.

The positive mind understands this and whispers realistic truth to keep you in track with your inner joy. These are the programmed arrangements of the positive mind expecting you to always follow. Of course challenges to hinder this inner joy always surrounds the mind but your ability to identify this joy features among them and work with it leads to its durability.

You can let your inner joy control you instead of depression by first listening and then submitting to the right voice. By this, never listen to any ill energy or negative energy. You don't have to wait till you are sad or down before trying to find a way of being happy.

Make it a routine just as you do other basic things. Depression comes when you don't except therefore get so connected to your positive mind enough to keep that inner joy fresh to be strong enough in hindering any form of depressed state. Invest in your joy. Allow your joy control you at every time.

You might wonder how you can probably let your joy be of control, you listening to your positive mind at all times is one of it. It is an emotion of positive energy connected to the positive mind that whispers to you. Therefore, it involves you with physical energy that speaks peace of mind. This joy gets you involves with things that calms your mental mind'

The positivity isn't there to hurt you. It is not just concern with that which you feel is your joy but what it knows is capable of pleasing your insight positively. It is however right to say that once you are connected to it, you are at the right track, its ok to be selfish for your inner peace to be preserved. It wouldn't lead you to become depressed later no, instead it balances your existence and that of your environment and involvement with people. Mind you, being selfish isn't about having to hurt someone but always ready to kick that energy wanting to corrupt your joy.

Your inner joy affects your physical movement. When you allow your inner joy act, you become relax with no troubled mind. You might be stressed, anxious or wanting something but your joy remains. Just as depression does, you try to communicate and do other things but it persist same thing applied to the positive side. It is left for you to decide, follow your joy or give room to depression. Do thing that keeps your mind in the best mood and when it comes to relationship, evaluate and listen. Surround yourself with positivity and at a time, it becomes completely part of you. You get to a stage were by you only think of positivity.

One good thing about inner joy is that you start developing positive attributes that could involve putting smile on peoples face. You find yourself doing things that increases your joy consistently. At one point or the other we get upset with someone and it is so because you can't control everyone to act as your mind wants or do what you think is right. Your positive mind knows this and won't allow them get in the way with your joy because you are connected to it.

Sometimes, when you walk with just physical attribute, you think you are at the right part but it later end in depression. Because is not from the inside, there is probability of making mistakes that looks like happiness in the beginning and then in a flash is gone. You see your friends enjoying that thing which you have always wanted it could be money, child, power e.t.c. having all this is not the problem, but the consequence you will face later if you just jump into it because you feel your friends are happy therefore you should be happy. That happiness that comes with what you see are temporal and cannot be described as joy because joy endures forever. Of course your positive mind wants to always preserve your inner joy therefore if it becomes one of the thing to keep that your inner joy alive it works towards it in a way that doesn't have to get you into depression later.

CHAPTER 4: AN EASY GAME MAINTAIN IT.

You now know how your positive mind can help you fight depression when you listen, you know what joy you get thereafter, the next thing you want to look towards is maintaining them. It becomes very easy when you are concern about your wellbeing because once your mind is full of how well you can always appear before others and to yourself, you strive for the best. No matter what it cost or what you think you will lost, you can't give what you don't have.

Positivity and negativity are not compatible no matter how good the negative side wants to appear, it doesn't change the facts that it's negative. . Like said in chapter 3 you can become selfish when it is trying to rob you of your joy.

This is common with humans some people dwell so much in negativity that they now look for a way to pass it round so as to get into that bad space as them, now you are trying to maintain your joy while listening to your inner mind. You do not want this bad space people to corrupt your thinking which can later lead to depression so you kick them out no matter what it means to you or what you think you might lose.

This set of people could be close enough that you need them around like in work or could even be your family. Remember no matter what it cost you, your joy must not be tempered with. In other to maintain this positive aspect, you must move away from them. Keep listening even while moving away. Sometimes we tend to keep deaf ears because of the benefits we are getting or more, allowing those negativity to build up in mind forgetting that your positive mind is only concern about keeping your inner joy therefore it can't leave you stranded.

It is negativity that cumulates together to form depression. You know those attributes of happiness smiling, fun, engagements and many more positive things that always leaves your feelings calm. Once something that doesn't looks or sounds like the calming attributes try's to come in, must not be let in no matter how they seems to present themselves. When you are able to work with your positive mind, do what makes you happy as much as possible without the fear of anything. Your mind doesn't want you to get depressed therefore anything you are doing to be happy will not get you depressed in the future as long as you are working with the positive mind.

Maintaining this joy is better than having to consult anyone for advice against depression. When you start maintaining your joy by not letting anything or anybody contaminate it, the joy becomes enduring. It is true that in some cases, it is difficult to avoid some situations. Sometimes you need someone to talk to and share how you feel, you must always be ready to evaluate while considering your mental health. This helps to maintain your source of joy.

Maintaining this joy can mean to be very sensitive to even the slightest thing that might not matter in the ordinary sense. Things that people tend to ignore regularly thinking it doesn't matter. While your mind is guiding you, you physically fight to maintain your joy. You might say that depression can hit anytime even when you aren't engaging in anything bad or negative. Yes this happens but do you also remember when something gets awkward at times, then in your head you begin to make statements like 'had I known I would have done it this way or that way'. Especially in a situation where it begins to lead to a depressive state, this is the beginning of that depression. Listening to the wrong voice or mind. Maintaining this joy, you must therefore always ready at all time to implement what the mind has given. Not just anything you feel your mind tells you but that positive mind.

The most important thing to achieving a stable and healthy maintenance against depression is by investing in your peace of mind. Your mind tells you what to do, you then follow them appropriately, and spice it physically. You want to be with new people, you want to learn new things, you want to explore and many more instead of having to be entangled in negativity.

Every human have those mixed emotions that at one points or the other want them to do something that can lead to depression if not handled well. Like jealousy, it becomes evil when you add hatred to it instead of having to be calm and listen to your positive mind. Maybe all you need to do is to evaluate your effort for positive results too you need to be really be connected to this mind in other to live your very best life. When this start happening, you realize that there's another part of life to be very happy.

CHAPTER 5 DON'T STAY BROKE

Do you realize that remaining broke is another strong feelings that can curse depression in one's life? You want to be on a safer side then you must do the right thing to remain buoyant or become rich. The reason why this aspect is important, is the fact that you forever remain important to eve n your less friends.

You want your mental health to be stable and healthy, then get rich and get what you want because humans will remain humans. Everyone will only get involve or give their whole time to something they can benefit from and no rich wants to associate with a low class.

You are aware of this and you want it to favor you positively. You do not have business with the negativity it might have because you work with the positive mind therefore you just want to keep your inner joy afresh as always. It might not be friends, but can be any means to involve yourself with the best positive energy around you. Remember that you can't achieve this if you're empty. We talk about investing in your joy in chapter 4. To get the best result, make the best positive money you can.

First thing you must understand as human is that no one owes you anything not even the ones you love. Your happiness, joy and peace lies in your hands. Therefore you must work through financial freedom. Money solves almost all problems in life. You are entitled to your joy as well as entitled to your own money.

Once you become in control of some reasonable amount of money, and you listen, you begin to live your best life positively. You can use your money to command things in a particular way for your joy. As long as long as your positive mind won't make you make you hurt others dangerously as well as it protects you from being hurt too, then you are entitled to your own happiness and joy.

 Do not misunderstand this part, there are people who wants to get rich through any means no matter what it might cost them because they see what to be rich looks like without having to consult their positive mind. This is not the type of wealth that is been emphasized here because it can get you depressed at any slightest time therefore rendering your wealth useless.

One thing is to be rich another thing is to be able to enjoy your wealth without any trouble or depressed mind attached therefore you want the most positive money ever. One problem why people think they are poor is because of the inability to act upon that opportunity or idea that comes up in your head or at random times and to some, it's the problem of starting. The most basic things that works for anyone is, first implement that reoccurring idea in your head which you think you can do, then train yourself enough to be good at what you do because the zeal is there even if it requires patience just make sure that positivity rules.

Now, at that moments you can first identify what can possibly lead to a depressed mind, you know how it feels and what it means to be depressed, the next thing you want to do is to try avoiding this because yes it can be avoided, of which positivity is the key. By been positive, you adapt the listening skills in other to be connected to your positive mind at all times.

You implement it to your everyday life. At that, you began to develop this inner joy that makes you happy you don't want that feelings to go so you maintain it while having in mind that humans are humans so the only way to balance this to fit your mental health is to be rich.

Once you are capable enough to implement this attributes discussed in this book, then you should be rest assured that what so ever depression that seems difficult to handle shouldn't be a problem to you because it will definitely be lifted as quick as possible as negativity and positivity don't go together. So therefore, you become a winner in the midst of depression.

CONCLUSION

This book opens your mind to most importantly those things many of us pays less attention to or see as nothing. Which unknown to us becomes the cause of a depressed state. Although depression is something that can happen anytime, the chapter two of this book made us to understand that depression can be avoided once you have possessed the power to listen, listen to that positive mind.

People like to feed on other people's weakness not minding where it later leads the person to thereafter that is why you must not let that happen by remaining broke which the last chapter tries to explain. At one point, you try to feel comfortable with yourself by engaging yourself with businesses, good jobs e.t.c. it only becomes a problem when you choose to remain in such position because it can likely mess with your mental health in anyway.

This book will make you understand that the best way to overcome such is by listening therefore giving you access to a lasting inner joy.